PATTERNS OF LIFE

Getting Around

Getting
Around

Daphne Butler

RSVP
RAINTREE
STECK-VAUGHN
P U B L I S H E R S
The Steck-Vaughn Company

Austin, Texas

Published by Raintree Steck-Vaughn Publishers,
an imprint of Steck-Vaughn Company

Design: SPL Design

Library of Congress Cataloging-in-Publication Data

Butler, Daphne. 1945–
    Getting around / Daphne Butler
       p. cm. -- (Patterns of Life)
    Includes index.
    Summary: Describes how different animals, birds, insects, and
humans get around and the physical characteristics that govern
how they move.
    ISBN 0-8172-4202-3
    1. Animal locomotion--Juvenile literature. [1. Animal
locomotion.] I. Title. II. Series: Butler, Daphne, 1945–
Patterns of life.
QP301.B94   1996
591.1'852--dc20
                                   95-15547
                                      CIP
                                      AC

Printed and bound in Singapore
by KHL Printing Co Pte Ltd
1 2 3 4 5 6 7 8 9 0   99 98 97 96 95

Photographs: Zefa except for
Robert Harding (cover, title page, 12t)

Contents

6

When you were a baby, all you
could do was wiggle and roll.
Soon you learned how to crawl.

Then you learned to stand on two
feet. Before long you were walking.

Your strong legs have joints at your
ankles, knees, and hips. Muscles
help these legs and feet bend.

You can walk, dance, run, and do all
kinds of exercise.

Slithering and Sliding

Some animals have no arms or legs. They often move along by slithering and sliding.

Snakes wiggle along. Sometimes
they move sideways on the sand.

Snails move, too. They shuffle
their bodies on a mat of slime.
This leaves a trail behind them.

11

Two Legs

Birds have two legs, just like people. Some have long legs for wading in water. Others have webs between their toes for swimming.

Birds' feet have three long toes that point forward. One toe points backward. With these toes they can rest easily on twigs and branches.

How many toes do you have?

Moving on Four

Many animals have four legs, but they don't have any arms or wings.

Many four-legged animals move very fast on long slender legs. They run much faster than people.

Other animals move more slowly. They may have shorter legs or heavier bodies.

15

Hooves and Paws

Some animals have hooves that are hard, like your toenails. Each foot can have a single hoof. Or it can be split into two or four hooves.

Other animals have paws. Their toes are round and soft. The toe has a pad under it, like a cushion. Each toe has a claw at the end.

What kind of toes does the turtle have? What kind of toes does the chameleon have?

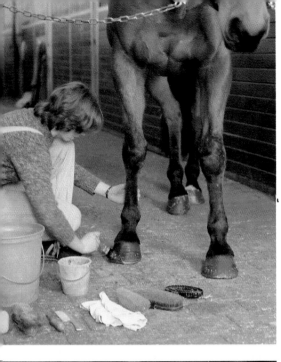

Six Legs or More

The spider has eight legs and a pair of spinnerets. The crab has eight legs and a pair of pincers with claws.

The caterpillar has three pairs of legs and five pairs of false legs.

The millipede has many legs.

Can you find these animals and their legs in the pictures?

Butterflies have two pairs of wings. They each have a front pair and a back pair of wings.

20

Birds have one pair of wings and a tail. They can spread their feathers to help them fly.

Great Swimmers

Animals with flippers are slow and clumsy on land. When they dive into water, they are swift and powerful swimmers.

Can you swim?

Do you think you can swim as fast
as the seal?

Underwater Creatures

Fish spend all of their lives under water. They swim by wagging their tails and steer with their fins.

Some underwater creatures are mammals. This dolphin comes up to the surface to breathe air.

Do you know how fish breathe?

Travel Anywhere

People can travel through the air like birds and in the ocean like fish.

26

They do this by using special equipment.

What other equipment or vehicles do people make to help them travel?

birds Warm-blooded animals with two legs and two wings. They usually fly. Birds hop or walk when they are on the ground. Some have webbed feet for paddling or swimming. A few, like penguins or ostriches, cannot fly.

fish Cold-blooded animals that live underwater and breathe through gills. They get around by wagging their tails and steering with their fins.

insects Small animals that usually have six legs and two or four wings for flying. Their bodies are divided into three parts.

mammals Warm-blooded animals that usually live on land and have two or four legs. Some, like whales, live underwater and 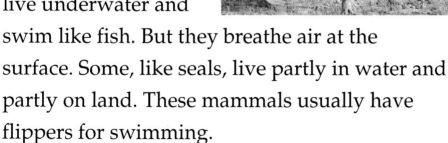 swim like fish. But they breathe air at the surface. Some, like seals, live partly in water and partly on land. These mammals usually have flippers for swimming.

29

Index

Mm
mammals 25, 29
millipede 19
muscles 9

Pp
paws 16
people 13, 15, 26, 27

Rr
roll 7
run 9, 15

Ss
shuffle 11
sliding 10
slithering 10

snails 11
snakes 11
spider 19
swimmers 22
swimming 13

Tt
tail 21, 24
toes 13, 16
travel 26

Ww
wading 13
wagging 24
walking 7
wiggle 7, 11
wings 14, 20, 21

31